FLOCK

Flock: Lead your tribe. Feed your team. Protect your people.

Copyright © 2020 Tom Roy

All rights reserved. No part of this book may be used or reproduced by any means, graphic, electronic, mechanical, including photocopying, recording, taping, or by any information storage retrieval system without the written permission of the author except in the case of brief quotations embodied in critical articles and reviews.

> Scripture quotations marked (ESV) are from the ESV® Bible (The Holy Bible, English Standard Version®), copyright © 2001 by Crossway, a publishing ministry of Good News Publishers. Used by permission. All rights reserved.

> Scriptures marked (NIV) are taken from the Holy Bible, New International Version®, NIV®. Copyright © 1973, 1978, 1984, 2011 by Biblica, Inc.™ Used by permission of Zondervan. All rights reserved worldwide. www.zondervan.com The "NIV" and "New International Version" are trademarks registered in the United States Patent and Trademark Office by Biblica, Inc.™

> Scripture quotations marked (TLB) are taken from The Living Bible copyright © 1971. Used by permission of Tyndale House Publishers, a Division of Tyndale House Ministries, Carol Stream, Illinois 60188. All rights reserved.

ISBN: 9798645083878

A Publication of Tall Pine Books

|| *tallpinebooks.com*

*Printed in the United States of America

FLOCK

LEAD YOUR TRIBE. FEED YOUR TEAM.
PROTECT YOUR PEOPLE.

TOM ROY

Tall Pine

DEDICATION

This book is dedicated to the faithful men and women of UPI and their spouses.

First, the pioneers. Phil Menzie had the administrative skills that allowed me to do what God had called me to do. He was always available and his support enabled UPI to move beyond infancy. For many years Marlyn French also offered her organizational skills behind the scenes.

Tim Cash, Don Gordon, and Brian Hickerson took a chance on a young leader and moved to Indiana to join the ministry. Tim took on the challenge of becoming the USA director, shaping and sharpening the division. Don's heart for discipleship took the ministry deeper into God's Word. Brian poured his heart into the military division, and along with his wife, Jo, kept the ministry running smoothly. They have each moved on to other ministries, but their fingerprints remain, and UPI is better for it.

What can I say about Glenn and Connie Johnson,

humble servants who are now in the presence of the Lord. Thank you, good and faithful servants.

A special thank you to the Board of Directors, especially Randy Swanson who chaired the board for many years. Each one brought wisdom, faith, integrity and balance, surrounding each decision with prayer. A thank you also to the part time staff and many volunteers over the years.

Mickey Weston took a leap of faith to leave coaching and join our band of renegades. He led the international division and now he is the executive director, leading the current staff. God continues to take UPI to new levels under his leadership.

Brian Hommel brings his passion, energy, and depth to the ministry as the Southwest director and Tony Graffanino adds his strength, wisdom and leadership on both sides of the country.

Terry Evans brings a rich understanding of theology and technology to UPI. Welcome to Angie Howett, Luke Hochever, and Tyler Keele, the newest staff members. I look forward to seeing their personal contributions to the ministry. For more information about UPI, visit www.upi.org.

I am grateful to each one for believing in UPI and for allowing me to be part of their lives. This book is dedicated to them.

SPECIAL THANKS

Without the love, encouragement and dedication of my wife Carin and daughters Amy and Lindsay this book could not have been written. All three speak life into me and love me unconditionally. Forever grateful!

A special shout out to Carin. On Aug 29, 2020 we will have been married 50 years. Hours and years of laughs, tears, travel, ministry and living a vagabond life style. She sacrificed much of herself to promote and care for me. She took the role of two parents as I travelled, brought our girls up in the love of Christ, gave up her own identity to allow me to lead and she even served as an editor of my books! I love you! So much of what God has done and is doing is because of you. THANK YOU!

> "If you think you are a leader and no one is following you, you are only taking a walk."
>
> AFGHAN PROVERB

A leader without a flock isn't a leader but a loner. A flock does not have to be a massive organization, a large congregation, or a world class team. A flock might be a small group, a few humble mentees or your own children.

CONTENTS

Foreword	xiii
A Note from the Author	xvii
1. Shepherds	1
2. Style	7
3. Evaluate	11
4. Heart	17
5. Essentials	23
6. Diversity	33
7. Develop	41
Mid-Book Jokes	51
8. Wolves	53
9. Education	57
10. R.E.A.L.	65
11. Responsive	69
12. Engaged	75
13. Authentic	81
14. Loyalty	87
15. Challenge	95
About the Author	97
Also by Tom Roy	99
End Notes	101

FOREWORD

How do you begin to describe an individual who has dramatically impacted your life and helped to change your life's trajectory? I have been privileged for the last 30 plus years to follow in the footsteps of Tom Roy as he led the ministry of Unlimited Potential Inc. In 1980, as a visionary, Tom stepped out in faith and began a work that no one had done before. Passionate for the game of baseball and for the Lord he serves, Tom began to take the gospel through the game of baseball to every corner of the world. John C. Maxwell has stated; "Leadership is not about titles, positions or flowcharts. It's about one life influencing another." This describes Tom's impact on me and the life that he continues to live.

My first overseas trip with Tom was to South Korea in 1986. Tom has a way of making everyone around him feel at ease. He leads with confidence and humility. He is respectful, compassionate, and an incredible encourager. I have never been with someone who has the ability to connect so easily with others. Learning from his example, I was inspired to begin leading trips with UPI during baseball's off-seasons. Tom taught me to love people of other cultures and how to effectively teach the game and communicate God's love in places I never would have dreamed I would go.

Tom not only leads well, but he also knows how to feed those under his care. Drawing from life experiences, Tom models how to be humble, vulnerable, and honest. As a trusted mentor he shares both successes and mistakes, and lessons learned from both. When I came on staff with UPI in 1996, I was encouraged by Tom to "put my fingerprints" on the international side of the ministry that I was to direct. He fueled my passion for the world and challenged me to keep my focus on others. He also attempted to teach me to keep life in balance through laughter. An entire book could be written about his sense of humor and the multiple pranks he has played on others and that have been played on him, deservedly. In all ways, this is a man who knows how to feed another's soul.

Of all the compliments that I could possibly give Tom, the greatest would be that he has represented Jesus well to me. Tom lives and loves from his core beliefs. As a shepherd protects his flock from predators, I have always known that Tom has had my back in any and every situation. He expresses his belief in me and has seen things in me that I did not have the faith to see. He entrusted the UPI leadership into my hands several years ago without hesitation and has since been my most faithful cheerleader. As a man of integrity, he shares the truth in love with me, but always with the focus towards learning.

"Shepherd Coach" is the perfect name for Tom Roy. He is a proven shepherd of the flocks that he has served: whether they be his family, the teams he has coached, the UPI ministry or the multitudes of individuals he has influenced over the course of his life. I am privileged to be considered one of his flock!

—MICKEY WESTON
Executive Director, *Unlimited Potential Inc.*
Former MLB Pitcher '89-'93

A NOTE FROM THE AUTHOR

I'm so glad you're here! It's exciting to see leaders like you who desire to lead with Kingdom principles. So many organizations allow current culture to lead and define direction. Whatever your flock, you, my friend, can define your culture. Join me as we walk through culture change toward shepherd leadership.

With so many books on leadership, why add one more? Good question. Some of you have more experience, education, and expertise than I do. I've read quite a few of your books and gained valuable insight. I am grateful for mentors and key people who have poured into my life.

This book comes from more than fifty years of personal failure and success as a leader. I am constantly reminded we are all in process, and I am still learning. I believe the focus of this book is different from most. My heartbeat is for Christian leaders to lead like a shepherd; the Chief Shepherd. I can tell you I haven't always led like Jesus. At times I have allowed pressure, ignorance, and pride to get in the way. This book is intended to shed light on what I've learned so you can lead your flock like a shepherd.

> "With upright heart he shepherded them and guided them with his skillful hand." (Psalms 78:72 ESV)

> "Be shepherds of God's flock that is under your care, watching over them—not because you must, but because you are willing, as God wants you to be; not pursuing dishonest gain, but eager to serve." (1 Peter 5:2 NIV)

> *"The focus of this book is leading like a shepherd—the Chief Shepherd."*

1

SHEPHERDS

EARLY IN THE ministry of UPI, I was asked to speak to a group of pro baseball coaches at the AAA level. At first I had no idea what to speak on, but finally settled on Jesus' words about shepherds from John 10. As I got into it, I noticed the coaches were locked in. I realized many of them saw themselves in the story and I knew I had hit on something important. That day shaped my entire approach to leadership.

Let's listen in to the words of the Chief Shepherd:

> "'Very truly I tell you Pharisees, anyone who does not enter the sheep pen by the gate, but climbs in by some other way, is a thief and a robber. The one who enters by the gate is the shepherd of the sheep. The gatekeeper opens the gate for him, and the sheep listen to his voice. He calls his own sheep by name and leads them out.

When he has brought out all his own, he goes on ahead of them, and his sheep follow him because they know his voice. But they will never follow a stranger; in fact, they will run away from him because they do not recognize a stranger's voice.'

Jesus used this figure of speech, but the Pharisees did not understand what he was telling them. Therefore Jesus said again, 'Very truly I tell you, I am the gate for the sheep. All who have come before me are thieves and robbers, but the sheep have not listened to them. I am the gate; whoever enters through me will be saved. They will come in and go out, and find pasture. The thief comes only to steal and kill and destroy; I have come that they may have life, and have it to the full.

I am the good shepherd. The good shepherd lays down his life for the sheep. The hired hand is not the shepherd and does not own the sheep. So when he sees the wolf coming, he abandons the sheep and runs away. Then the wolf attacks the flock and scatters it. The man runs away because he is a hired hand and cares nothing for the sheep. I am the good shepherd; I know my sheep and my sheep know me—just as the Father knows me and I know the Father—and I lay down my life for the sheep.'" (John 10:1-15 NIV)

Did you read that? Yes, I know some of you have read it before and you may have skimmed through it. Just in case you missed it, I want you to notice there are four types of shepherds mentioned by the Chief Shepherd.

- The stranger
- The thief/robber
- The hired hand
- The True Shepherd

Are your sheep listening to you? If not, maybe you have become a *stranger* to them and they are seeking other voices. You may need to get reacquainted. Listening to them and showing interest in them is your antidote.

What about the one Jesus calls the *thief* or *robber*? Some leaders are only in it for what they can get out of it. Maybe it's the title or maybe it's the money. Either way, your sheep know you are only there for their wool or their mutton. When the sheep get restless, thieves will not lead the sheep to greener pastures; they will move on to greener pastures themselves. There are quite a few thief leaders out there.

Or maybe you are the *hired hand.* You put in your time and you do what is expected of you. You watch the numbers or the scoreboard. You are results oriented but your heart's not in it. You have no personal interest in the flock. Sheep come and go; they are a commodity to you. Some well-intentioned leaders fall into this category. They buy into the philosophy that it's a bad idea to become emotionally attached to employees. Trust and teamwork will suffer under this style of leadership.

A few leaders are true shepherd leaders. These are the leaders who are willing to put the needs of the sheep first. They lead by example. They are not afraid to step into the role of a sheep and do the worst job in the flock. They protect the flock from danger and provide for the needs of the flock.

> "Goodness is about character — integrity, honesty, kindness, generosity, moral courage, and the like. More than anything else, it is about how we treat other people."
>
> DENNIS PRAGER, RADIO SHOW HOST

Let's zoom in closer on what a good shepherd leader looks like:

1. Shepherd leaders realize they have been given a specific assignment. They follow the Chief Shepherd as they lead others, knowing He is their source of power and wisdom. They are aware they are sheep themselves who have been asked to wear shepherd's clothing.
2. Shepherd leaders realize they have been given specific abilities and opportunities to carry out the shepherding task.
3. Shepherd leaders realize their flock is particular to their calling.
4. Shepherd leaders realize they are a target. The enemy hates shepherds and will send in 'thieves' to steal, kill and destroy the flock.
5. Shepherd leaders realize they need to fight for their flock God's way. (Galatians 6:1)

6. Shepherd leaders realize the job can get messy. Tending a flock can be a dirty job.
7. Shepherd leaders realize each one in the flock has value. The shepherd's role is to help the flock reach their potential with godly guidance.
8. Shepherd leaders realize it is important to listen and learn while tending the flock.
9. Shepherd leaders realize they need to lead their flock in finding spiritual nourishment.
10. Shepherd leaders protect the flock from danger. If one of the flock insists on going their own way, this may involve breaking the legs and carrying the sheep.
11. Shepherd leaders understand the need for rest. Shepherding is a grind. They realize their flock needs rest as well.
12. Shepherd leaders are committed to putting the needs of their flock above their own.

DISCLAIMER: Jesus is the Chief Shepherd and the only true shepherd leader. This leader falls far short of his standard, but will continue to press on toward that standard.

Former left tackle for the Green Bay Packers and great friend Ken Ruettgers, introduced me to the following analogy. Most of us are familiar with checkers and chess. Both games are played on the same board and both involve moving game pieces. But there is a major difference between the two.

In the game of checkers, the goal is to jump you and king me. Chess is different. It's a game of strategy and the player is always thinking several moves ahead. The goal is to protect the king!

Shepherd leaders do not use their flock as stepping stones to move up the ladder and become "kings." Shepherd leaders make kings. They are always looking ahead, keeping their eyes on the King, the Chief Shepherd, while feeding and caring for their flock. Shepherd leaders do everything they can to strategically place their people in positions where they can exercise their gifts and succeed. Shepherd leaders value their flock; they understand that every person and every position is important.

"Shepherd leaders make kings."

2
STYLE

LEADERSHIP STYLES VARY. The following are some of the most popular leadership styles. You may identify with some of these styles.

1. Autocratic Leadership

This leadership style is centered on the boss.

2. Democratic Leadership

This leadership style involves subordinates in decision-making.

3. Strategic Leadership

This leadership style is not limited to those at the top of the organization, but incorporates others at various levels.

4. Transformational Leadership

Unlike other leadership styles, transformational leadership is all about initiating change in organizations, groups, self and others.

5. Team Leadership

This style of leadership involves the creation of a vivid picture of a team's future, where it is heading and what it will stand for. The vision inspires and provides a strong sense of purpose and direction.

6. Cross-Cultural Leadership

This form of leadership normally exists where there are various cultures in the society. This leadership has also industrialized as a way to recognize front-runners who work in the contemporary globalized market.

7. Facilitative Leadership

This leadership style is dependent on measurements and outcomes rather than a skill, although it takes much skill to master. The effectiveness of a group is directly related to the efficacy of its process. If the group is high functioning, the facilitative leader uses a light hand on the process.

8. Laissez-faire Leadership

This leadership style gives authority to employees. Departments or subordinates are allowed to work as they choose with minimal or no interference.

9. Transactional Leadership

This leadership style maintains or continues the status quo. It is also the leadership that involves an exchange process, whereby followers get immediate, tangible rewards for carrying out the leader's directives.

10. Coaching Leadership

This leadership style involves teaching and supervising followers. A coaching leader is highly operational in settings where continuous improvement in performance is required for results.

11. Charismatic Leadership

In this style of leadership, the leader manifests his or her revolutionary power. Charisma does not mean sheer behavioral change. It actually involves a transformation of followers' values and beliefs. Charismatic leaders tend to have powerful personalities and attract huge followings. Examples of such leaders are Barack Obama and Oprah Winfrey.

12. Visionary Leadership

This form of leadership involves leaders who recognize that the methods, steps and processes of leadership are all obtained with and through people.[1]

13. Servant Leadership

"Servant leadership is a leadership philosophy in which an individual interacts with others—either in a management or fellow employee capacity—with the aim of achieving authority rather than power. The system embodies a decentralized organizational structure."[2]

My hope is to challenge these traditional ways of thinking about leadership which inform your style. You've picked up this book, so my guess is that's your hope as well. It shows you have a desire to be a man or woman who leads like a shepherd. Your flock is important to you. Your flock is also important to God and he chose you to lead them. You have the opportunity to influence the destiny of each one following you. Let's examine the methods, tools, and resources needed to accomplish that goal.

> "No matter what ship you are boarding today...hardship, fellowship, discipleship, friendship...they all need a captain called leadership."
>
> JEAN-LUC GODARD

3
EVALUATE

"Keep watch over yourselves and all the flock of which the Holy Spirit has made you overseers. Be shepherds of the church of God, which he bought with his own blood. I know that after I leave, savage wolves will come in among you and will not spare the flock." (Acts 20:28-29 NIV)

A SHEPHERD IS one who tends to the sheep; who leads from the front; who draws the sheep to himself. A sheepherder is someone who drives sheep and herds from the back of the flock. These are two very different methods of caring for sheep and two very different leadership styles.

Let's start by emphasizing the need we have to evaluate ourselves and others to see if we are qualified to lead. A good look in the mirror is valuable. Take a good look and ask yourself who you see. Then ask yourself who your sheep see. Is there a difference between the two? Authenticity is a great place to begin. Sheep can see right through us, so being transparent is essential before we put on the shepherd's robe.

I believe this begins with humility. We don't need to wear a facade of self-confidence. God has provided us with opportunities and placed us in positions of influence. He equips the leader with the talent and ability to do the job and trusts his sheep to us. Keeping that in proper perspective helps prevent an attitude of pride.

> "The balance between necessary, self-confidence, and arrogant self-righteousness can be a challenge at times, particularly in the world of sport where we are judged by our performance."
>
> STUART WEIR

Good shepherds are diligent, dependable, and brave. They even risk their lives to protect the flock. It is not a calling for the weak of heart. Let's evaluate some important aspects of shepherd leadership.

COURAGE

Courage is a mainstay of good leadership. To show courage, as my friend Sam Marsonek taught me, Shepherd Leaders need to:

- **Reject Passivity.** The Messiah knew His purpose and moved toward the Cross.

- **Accept Responsibility.** Don't be afraid of assignments and understand that failure can be a teacher.
- **Serve Endlessly.** Phililippians 2 lays out a lifelong attitude of service that we would benefit from reading and duplicating.

Zig Zigler has said F.E.A.R. has two meanings: "Forget Everything And Run" or Face Everything And Rise." The choice is yours. Are you brave enough to say that no matter the consequences you are ready to face the challenge and make the right choice?

EVALUATION

Part of evaluation is asking tough questions like:

- Am I ready for the battles ahead?
- Am I equipped to be an influencer?

There is a difference between power and influence. For example, military leaders need to develop trust in those they lead. In life or death situations, it makes a difference if those under their command are following because of rank or because of trust.

The same is true for every leader. It's one thing to have a title and authority. It's another thing to gain the trust of the flock you lead. Shepherd leaders are more interested in godly influence than using power to create submissive drones.

FURTHER EVALUATION

Further evaluation might include questions like:

- Am I leading because of the power it gives or am I truly influencing others?
- Am I interested in the rewards of leadership or in seeing growth in the flock?

There is a difference. As a coach, I understand the need to win, but individual and team *growth* is just as important. Combined growth means that down the road the team will do better than they are doing today. Why? Because they will be listening, caring, and learning from their mistakes. These are principles they will carry through their lives.

- Am I task-oriented or people-oriented?

There is nothing wrong with being a task-oriented leader, but you will probably need to get an assistant who is interested in caring for the flock. A head coach and assistant coach who are both task-oriented may produce a team that's starving for relational support. Know your strengths and staff accordingly.

- Am I motivated by production or principles?

Shepherd leaders tend to be more principle-oriented, so they are wise to work beside others with production goals to complement their calling.

- Am I leading out of fear or caring?

Fear can be a great motivator, but not for the long term. Caring seems to have a little more hang time. Fear is real and can lead to poor decisions. Shepherd leaders will face wolves that threaten the flock. Leading from fear can pass fear on to the flock and make for restless sheep. Fear that reaches you should stop with you if you care for your flock.

- Am I leading to use people or serve people?

Some leaders use people. They see people as necessary tools to accomplish their goals. That works for a while, but eventually people get used up and leaders are forced to look for people to replace them. Servant leaders see those they lead as valuable, not dispensable. They find ways to let people know they are valued.

- Am I a leader or a manager?

Warren Bennis has likely done more to popularize this distinction than anyone else. He wrote in *Learning to Lead: A Workbook on Becoming a Leader* that, "There is a profound difference between management and leadership, and both are important. To manage means to bring about, to accomplish, to have charge of or responsibility for, to conduct. Leading is influencing, guiding in a direction, course, action, opinion. The distinction is crucial." And in one of his most famous lines, he added, "Managers are people who do things right and leaders are people who do the right thing."

These are questions to get you started on the evaluation process. There is a saying in business circles that is worth considering: "What can be measured can be managed." There is some truth to this in shepherd leadership, but so much of what you do will only be evaluated in eternity. This doesn't mean we shouldn't evaluate our leadership or work hard at stewarding what has been entrusted to us. It means the final evaluation belongs to the Chief Shepherd. Jesus sees your investment!

Remember, you can spend your life anywhere. The question is where will you *invest* it?

"People buy into the leader before they buy into the vision."

JOHN MAXWELL

4

HEART

THE FOUR PILLARS OF A SHEPHERD LEADER

> "For he is our God and we are the people of his pasture, the flock under his care. " (Psalm 95:7 ESV)

SHEPHERDS in ancient Israel likely worked with, among others, the broadtail Syrian variety of sheep, which have large fatty tails and a thick fleece. The rams of this breed are horned, and the ewes are not. These docile animals are easily led and completely at the mercy of their environment and predators.

"Shepherds also cared for goats. The goats were uniformly black or brown. Their long, flapping ears easily got torn on thorns and briar bushes as they clambered on rocky hillsides and grazed on shrubbery. The shepherd faced the ongoing challenge of teaching the sheep and goats to obey his commands. Even so, good shepherds took tender care of the animals in their charge, even giving them names to which they would respond." [1]

Good shepherds want to grow in knowledge and lead with passion. They care deeply about those they lead and seek wisdom each day. Shepherd leaders are called to lead, feed, care and protect the sheep.

LEAD

Shepherd Leaders lead from the front. Leaders, like Jesus, draw people to themselves. You have most likely experienced this. If not, you will need to walk first into the mystery of the unknown with courage. Shepherd leaders may have experience, but they will attempt to promote Christ rather than self (see Phil. 3:4-9).

> "The heart of man plans his way, (the leader's responsibility) but the Lord establishes his steps (God's responsibility)." (Proverbs 16:9 ESV)

"If you see someone driving a flock from the back rather than leading from the front, he is probably not a shepherd; he is most likely a butcher!"

FEED

Shepherd leaders feed the flock. You lead your flock to green pastures and expose them to the latest techniques and greatest biblical principles. You may ask, "What if they get too good and leave?" A better question might be, "What if they remain ignorant and stay?" You can count the number of seeds in an orange, but you cannot count the number of oranges and orange groves in a seed. Invest in others!

CARE

Shepherd leaders are about relationships. One key to good relationships is knowing God is in control. My daily personal motto is "It's great to be alive because God is in control!" The result of this is I can focus on others and gladly care for their needs. Shepherd leadership is a culture of true caring. The world defines culture by achievement. A shepherd leader lives from the heart of Jesus. (Matt. 6:21)

PROTECT

Shepherd leaders protect. Wolves are out there. Without you, the flock is vulnerable. We will discuss this topic in further detail later in the book. Courage can be contagious.

"Shepherd Leadership involves showing up, listening up, reading up and giving up."

It's amazing the kind of things that can happen if we just show up. Add to that a commitment to listening to people. Be hungry to read all you can to improve your leadership, especially the Bible, the world's greatest leadership manual. Apply what you learn. Giving up means doing your best, accepting responsibility, and trusting God with the outcome.

One thread that you will see throughout this book is my philosophy of, "make kings instead of trying to be the king." Jesus calls it making disciples. This means caring for your flock by investing in them, no matter their current state of mind. Sheep need a leader.

You might ask, "But what if I make mistakes as a leader?"

I have a heart for developing young leaders and preparing them for the challenges ahead. Seeing them lead from the culture they live in with the truth of God's Word matters to me. I can tell you, making mistakes and experiencing misunderstandings is all part of the process.

Be prepared to handle mistakes with humility and compassion. Making mistakes is a great way to learn so the same mistakes are not repeated. Your flock is watching, and they will learn how to handle failure by your example. If the mistakes are unethical, illegal, or immoral, there needs to be an investigation into why they occured. In a later chapter we will discuss the way people think and process decision making in these matters.

For shepherd leaders, perfection is not the goal. Only One was perfect and we are not Him. Rather, we need to focus on attitudes and processes. It is wise to remember that when someone makes a mistake, a shepherd leader never shames the sheep, but empowers them to learn from failure. The goal of the shepherd leader is to make great future leaders, which means allowing them to fail, to learn, to grow. It means believing in them and their potential.

Not every leadership style embraces errors the way a shepherd leader does. It takes effort to change old ways of leading. But shepherd leadership can be embraced by everyone. Why? Because it is the leadership style Jesus taught and modeled.

We are each called to lead well in our current position in life. Don't wait for someday. Do it now! We are called to do our best to the glory of God. No matter what you are doing, someone is watching, and that makes you a leader. The world is looking for people with vision and character. We are all called to lead, feed, care and protect in some capacity.

INTROSPECTION

To understand what it means to be a shepherd leader will require a time of introspection and reflection. Look around to see who is watching you and looking to you for leadership. Evaluate who you are and what you believe your role is in their lives. Be sure to measure yourself against the truth of the Word of God.

Introspection can be lonely and it can expose painful realities. If you want to grow as a shepherd leader, you will need to understand it is often more of an attitude than a system. It's an intentional process of caring about, feeding, protecting and providing for other people. The following are some of the challenges ahead:

1. Giving up control but not giving up.
2. Trusting but being responsible.
3. Resting but being active.
4. Running the race before us but with patience.

5

ESSENTIALS

MISSION STATEMENT

A VERY IMPORTANT follow up to introspection is the development of a personal mission statement. What do I mean by that? I mean writing out your own personal philosophy, purpose and mission. That will include asking, "Why do I do what I do and why do I do it the way I do it?" This may start out as multiple paragraphs, but eventually, you should be able to narrow it down to a clear, concise statement.

If you read my last book, *Shepherd Coach*, you understand that a lot of my early leadership tools were developed as a high school and college coach. My first full time job was as head baseball coach at a public high school. It was in that context that I realized the need to have a personal mission statement. From my mission I could measure and determine success. Without a mission, I had nothing to measure. Was I going to allow a group of fifteen to eighteen year old athletes to define success for me? Was the scoreboard the only thing that counted? After weeks of reflection I came up with the following:

"People are more important than programs; programs are more important than winning. Winning is important."

As a coach, I realized there were scoreboards in games as well as in life, and records were being kept. I wanted my players to be successful both on the scoreboard and in life. For many coaches, the scoreboard is the only definition of success. I prayed and decided there was more.

I was thrown into a position of leadership. People would be looking to me for guidance, direction, instruction, discipline, strategy and passion. How would I proceed? Once I had an understanding of my mission statement, the next step was to apply it to my situation. The beginning phase was to know my sheep, know my goals and know where growth was needed.

I felt it was very important to concentrate on each member of the team, both on and off the field. A coach is responsible for the quality of the program. A coach has an opportunity to influence the lives of the players. A team will not always score the most points in every sporting event. A true shepherd leader has to define and redefine what a win looks like.

A Leader's Direction Comes from the Chief Shepherd

Rick Warren said: "If you base your life on God's Word, the truth never changes. Truth is alway true. So if God says something was wrong 10,000 years ago, it was also wrong 500 years ago, it's wrong today, and will be wrong 1,000 years from today. I don't care what opinion polls or political correctness or the media says. If God says it's wrong, it's wrong. It always has been, and it always will be. If God says it is right, it will always be right. That is a solid foundation!"

The shepherd leader who makes decisions based on biblical truth will have a solid standard for decision making. I believe we need to listen to others but filter all voices through God's eternal wisdom.

A Leader's Identity Comes from the Chief Shepherd

Speaking of biblical truth, remember God's opinion of you is the truest opinion. Leaders are targets. There will always be doubters and critics. For some reason, God chose you to be a leader. He sees something in you. He sees what you can become. Shepherd leaders need to listen to the Chief Shepherd before anyone else.

A Shepherd Leader Needs to Know the Lay of the Land

As a leader, I had to evaluate my audience, tools, expectations and direction.

The players and the assistant coaches were my audience.

The tools I was given to work with were their skills and abilities. As the head coach, I was expected to develop their talents, grow their skills and produce success on the field. As a *shepherd* coach, my desire was to develop growth in them as individuals as well as athletes, and that helped determine my direction.

A Shepherd Leader Needs to be a Light

> "If you keep your light at table level, you'll illuminate the people around the table. If you keep it in the corner, you'll illuminate people who are in the corner. But if you lift that same light high, elevate it, put it on a pedestal, and make it visible, it will illuminate *everyone* in the room where it previously touched only a handful. The amount of light given is the same, but the elevated position of the light makes the light much more effective."
>
> RICK RENNER

I was put on a light stand! This shepherd leadership philosophy developed out of a need to understand people and care for them. Who was I to take on such a role? Insecurity is real. Even though we are called on to be shepherds, we all feel like sheep in shepherd's clothing. I felt I was way over my skis. This was a good place to be. I had to hit my knees.

Since my coaching days, I've added the idea of making kings rather than being king. Shepherd leadership starts with a passion for Jesus and a love for the people He has put under your care.

Shepherd Leaders Need to Rely on the Leading of the Holy Spirit

That still, small voice can show you best from good, God from self.

The Holy Spirit rarely shouts. When he speaks, it is usually when we slow down enough to listen. Often he speaks with a nudge rather than words. Sometimes something doesn't feel right. We need to step on the brakes before proceeding. Sometimes we need to right a wrong. Other times, the Holy Spirit leads us to do something out of the ordinary. When the Holy Spirit leads, the shepherd leader listens.

A Shepherd Leader Needs to Be a Good Learner

Another element I learned in those early days was the need to get good information to become the good teacher the sheep needed. I also realized that to be a good teacher I was responsible to be continually learning and not just repeating the same information. I needed to learn from every situation and person I encountered. A shepherd leader needs to be comfortable with authority, but humble enough to learn from anyone. Most importantly, I needed to measure my knowledge with the truth of God's Word. His truth needed to lead the way.

A Shepherd Leader Needs to be God Reliant

One of the biggest questions shepherd leaders need to answer is whether they will be self-reliant or God-reliant. As a young coach, I felt pretty good about my knowledge of the game of baseball, but had so much to learn about people and programs. More importantly, I had to humbly admit I needed help. Prayer became a large part of my coaching. I had to try to understand what God wanted and not just rely on what I knew. This practice has continued throughout my life as the founder and director of UPI. A shepherd leader needs to remember who placed him in leadership and who is in control.

A Shepherd Leader Needs to be Understanding

As a shepherd leader, empathy is a sign of maturity. Notice I did not say sympathy. **Sympathy** is a feeling and expression of concern for someone, often accompanied by a wish for them to be happier or better off. **Empathy** requires the ability to recognize the suffering of another person from their point of view and to openly share their emotions, including painful distress. Sympathy borders on pity. At its worst, sympathy suggests superiority. At its best, sympathy says you care.

> "People don't need you to feel sorry for them. They need you to feel sorry WITH them. Sympathy serves you well when it leads to empathy and compassion. Empathy

suggests shared emotion. Compassion suggests dirty hands."

DAN ROCKWELL, LEADERSHIP FREAK

To deeply empathize with someone shows you are willing to take a risk. When you show empathy, you may be misunderstood or maligned. But a shepherd leader attempts to understand and care for people, no matter what. You see your flock as *people*, not as *objects*. Your purpose is not to manipulate them or to see them as possessions that you can move like a chess piece.

In my early leadership years, I was insecure and thought my role was to tell everyone what I believed, making sure they saluted that flag. I was not as interested in what they believed or how they were doing. We will develop this idea further in a later chapter about teachable moments.

Part of Shepherd Leadership means:

- Understanding that your flock is made of real people
- Leading them by example
- Knowing their strengths and weaknesses
- Being transparent
- Asking them good questions
- Getting to know them deeply and understanding

what is important to them, not just what is important to you

Shepherd leadership is caring-based in its purest form. This means embracing, empathizing with and having compassion for the people around you. It means continued personal growth while growing others. It means shared values and purpose. Every person we encounter is a potential divine appointment. Look for the worth in others.

Shepherd Leaders Need to Understand what Healthy Sheep Look Like

It is the exception to find healthy teams, at least teams that are healthy every day. It seems there are always areas that need improvement. There are always things which need to be revisited and relearned. A shepherd leader needs to be alert for areas of dysfunction in the flock.

A healthy team/flock will:

- Know why they do what they do
- Follow because they care
- Be aligned in the area they function best
- Care about each other

When a team really likes each other, they work better together. They need to believe in a common cause, and if they don't believe in the cause, it may be time to look for another place for them to work.

To Lead We Need Other Leaders to Speak Into Our Lives

Howard Hendricks once said that we all need a Paul, a Timothy and a Barnabas in our lives.

- Paul is someone who teaches us.
- Timothy is someone we are teaching.
- Barnabas is someone who encourages us.

To continue to grow and be held accountable we need others to lead us. Books are great. But shepherd leaders need the wisdom of the Chief Shepherd, Jesus, as well as the insight, wisdom and knowledge of people who have gone before them and are willing to provide input and ask questions.

Who is your Paul, your Timothy and your Barnabas?

Shepherd Leaders Need to Pray

Anyone truly serious about becoming a shepherd leader had better be committed to prayer. Find a group of people who will commit to pray for you. The shepherd leader is a target. The evil one hates it when people become committed to the cause of Jesus.

Don't be naive. We are in a war and our enemy is not flesh and blood. Surround yourself with prayer and put on the armor of God because the arrows are coming!

> "Finally, be strong in the Lord and in the strength of his might. Put on the whole armor of God, that you may be able to stand against the schemes of the devil. For we do not wrestle against flesh and blood, but against the rulers, against the authorities, against the cosmic powers over this present darkness, against the spiritual forces of evil in the heavenly places. Therefore take up the whole armor of God, that you may be able to withstand in the evil day, and having done all, to stand firm. Stand therefore, having fastened on the belt of truth, and having put on the breastplate of righteousness, and, as shoes for your feet, having put on the readiness given by the gospel of peace. In all circumstances take up the shield of faith, with which you can extinguish all the flaming darts of the evil one; and take the helmet of salvation, and the sword of the Spirit, which is the word of God, praying at all times in the Spirit, with all prayer and supplication. To that end, keep alert with all perseverance, making supplication for all the saints." (Ephesians 6:10-18 ESV)

> "A good leader gets people to follow him because they want to, not because he makes them."
>
> TONY DUNGY

6

DIVERSITY

DID you know that worldwide it is estimated there are more than 1000 distinct breeds of sheep? There are more than 60 breeds in the United States alone. This is true of your flock as well. As a shepherd of people, you lead a diverse group. You have individuals with different temperaments, different interests, different backgrounds, different learning styles and different ways of communication.

You are called to shepherd the entire herd. Some will be compliant, others excitable. Get to know your flock. Learn who they are as people, what they care about and what motivates them. Observe how they learn and how they relate to each other.

Let's look at communication. Fifty years ago we communicated with people in other locations by using a telephone connected to a wall. Today our phones fit in our pockets and offer dozens of ways to communicate. Those of us who remember wall phones need to choose to learn new ways of communicating, or we will be left behind. You need to be able to hear what your flock is saying. You have wisdom to share and you need to communicate it in ways they understand.

Shepherding well takes wisdom and prayer.

1. **Pray** for your flock. Commit them to the Chief Shepherd and ask for wisdom, courage and direction to lead well.
2. **Purge** negative voices. Each of us has a personal 'board of directors' in our brain, including people who have influenced us over the years. Not all of them are good. Those voices that do not add value need to be voted off the board. Ask Jesus, the chairman of the board, to speak truth over those voices.
3. **Purpose** to listen to godly voices. From the early days of UPI, I purposely surrounded myself with people better than me. These were people who had wisdom and skills beyond my own. Seek out people with fresh ideas, those with creative thinking skills. Avoid the "we can't" or the "we've never done it this way" mentality.
4. **Provide** for your flock. Offer frequent training. Make sure they have everything they need to do their job. Be intentional about encouragement. Reward successes.

5. **Protect** your people from wolves. A wolf may look like a lamb but they are divisive and destructive. Be on the lookout for anyone who is not a team player, who is undermining your leadership or is disloyal to the organization.

A healthy flock shares the shepherd's vision. You will always face challenges. As a college coach, I was having a problem with a player who was not buying into my vision, and he was taking other players along with him. Finally, a wise friend told me, "Tom, you need to recruit kids that believe in what you believe in." He was right. Your team will work harder when they share your passion and vision. One person out of sync can ruin a good team. After much prayer, I made the difficult choice to protect the flock by keeping only those players who shared the same vision.

A healthy flock trusts their shepherd. The result will be unity and cooperation. Developing a healthy flock includes several elements:

1. **Carefully evaluate each person's talent and ability.** A healthy team is one in which each member knows what they do best and they contribute to the goal. It may be necessary to move individuals to other tasks to find the best fit for them. Each member should feel they add value.
2. **Observe how each one works with others.**

Encourage communication and teamwork. When the team wins, all win.

3. **Listen carefully to questions and ideas.** Create an open door policy where team members feel free to discuss ways to do things differently. Offer opportunities for team members to take ownership of projects.
4. **Create a family atmosphere.** Care about each team member as an individual and foster mutual caring on your team. Celebrate achievements and successes.
5. **Be open to discussing difficulties and dysfunction.** Don't be afraid of difficult discussions. Problems won't go away by themselves. Address them.
6. **Clearly articulate vision and goals.** Remind your team frequently why they are on your team and why it matters what they do.

Visuals Promote Vision

Focus equals follow. What we have discussed already is a lot for a leader to remember. Personally, I needed visuals to remind me of my responsibilities. If you had visited my office when I was the executive director of UPI, you would have seen a number of notes placed where I could see them. Those notes were continual reminders of my role in the lives of the flock God allowed me to lead. Your team needs visuals as well. You can't remind them enough of the mission, vision and values of your organization.

Leaders Hire Well

A healthy team begins with hiring. Look for people to join your flock with F. L. O.

- Faithful
- Loyal
- Obedient

"Your flock must be faithful to the cause, loyal to the team, and obedient to authority."

New members of the flock need to realize that they are joining a team and everyone needs to take ownership of their part. Not everyone has been called to be the shepherd. A shepherd leader desires the flock to succeed. For that to happen, each member needs to embrace their position, do their best and accept evaluation.

Shepherd leaders need to be willing and able to evaluate the flock. If one person on the team is failing on a consistent basis, the leader needs to be attentive and determine where that person fits best in the flock. Shepherd leaders care for the flock and that comes through in evaluations. Even correction can be expressed with kindness. Speak life into your flock!

"Instead, speaking the truth in love, we will grow to become in every respect the mature body of him who is the head, that is, Christ." (Ephesians 4:15)

Leaders Understand Their Position of Authority

A healthy flock respects authority, and that begins with you. God has appointed you to lead. That means doing what is best for the entire flock as well as for individuals. That can be a difficult balancing act, especially when you have individuals that buck your authority or need extra attention. It's up to you to keep the team on track and stay focused on your core values. A flock that knows their leader cares is more likely to respect the authority of their leader.

Allow me to illustrate from the game of baseball. You are a coach trying to build a healthy team. You desire to help each player discover their strengths and place them in positions where they can succeed. One of your players may want to hit in the fourth spot in the lineup. In baseball that's typically the spot for the best home run hitter who will hit the ball hard and drive in runs. As the coach, you know that player does not have the power to drive in runs, and it would hurt the team to place him in the four hole. You know they have speed and can bunt for a base hit, so you see them as a better leadoff hitter. They could also fill the number two spot because they are able to advance the runner. Your job is to help him understand his strengths and place him in the spot where he is best able to contribute to the team.

"Don't think you are better than you really are. Be honest in your evaluation of yourselves, measuring yourselves by the faith God has given us. Just as our bodies have many parts and each part has a special function, so it is with Christ's body. We are many parts of one body, and we all belong to each other." (Romans 12:3-6 NLT)

7
DEVELOP

"The LORD is my shepherd, I shall not want." (Psalm 23:1)

IN 1980, God put it on my heart to start an organization called Unlimited Potential Inc. (www.upi.org), an international ministry with professional baseball. It is still in operation today and thriving, in part because of what I am about to share with you.

For the first decade, UPI was a one man organization. It began in a corner of our basement with a card table and a push button phone. I was accountable to a board of directors, but I was the only one on staff. There were some outstanding opportunities and some tough times as well. The mission of UPI is to reach, teach, and train pro baseball players for the purpose of sending them into the world. The ministry was exploding and the workload was growing. It has been my privilege to lead this organization for the first 38 years, and I am forever grateful to the Lord for that opportunity.

About year nine of UPI, my father-in-law, Andy Brown, offered me some valuable advice. He had observed the growing ministry, the constant travel, and the toll it was taking on my family and my health, and he challenged me to add staff. He showed me from Scripture how Jethro encouraged Moses, his son-in-law, to seek help. Moses knew how to govern, but it was too much for him to govern alone.

> "Moses' father-in-law replied, 'What you are doing is not good. You and these people who come to you will only wear yourselves out. The work is too heavy for you; you cannot handle it alone. Listen now to me and I will give you some advice, and may God be with you... select capable men from all the people—men who fear God...That will make your load lighter, because they will share it with you. If you do this and God so commands, you will be able to stand the strain Moses listened to his father-in-law and did everything he said." (Excerpted from Exodus 18:7-24 NIV)

It was great advice and the ministry was about to launch into a growth process. Delegating and cooperating would be one of many valuable leadership lessons God provided through Scripture and through godly mentors.

In the early days of UPI, three divisions were defined; North America, International, and Discipleship. Since I was traveling more than 300 days a year, the first staff person hired was a *North American Director*. A few years later, UPI hired a *Director of Discipleship*, and an *International Director* came next. Hiring meant hours of mentoring and discipling these men, which was a great honor. The benefits of investing in them far outweighed the time involved.

One of the first things I told these men was that I wanted their fingerprints all over their division of the ministry. I did not want them to be mini-me. I wanted their personalities and gifts to define what their division would look like. Essentially, these men designed their divisions. There were general guidelines and ministry values, but I wanted their personal signature on everything they touched.

By the grace of God, that is what happened. Each division grew and each man faithfully produced lasting fruit. There were struggles along the way, but lives were influenced for eternity and God was honored. If it were not for these men and the others that have followed, UPI would not have thrived. It has been thrilling to see God work through each of them. Some of those early employees have since moved on to other ministries and they are still using their gifts to serve Jesus. Others continue to guide the ministry of UPI.

None of this would have been possible without a good office manager. Over the years, the administrative skills of Phil, Marlyn, Connie, Brian, and Jo were gold at running the office and keeping us all in line.

The primary blueprint I used in the process of preparing the staff is what I call **BE-SEE-FLEE-PLEA-BE**.

In a new environment it's normal for an employee to ask

what is expected of them. There were job descriptions and policies for each to follow, but in the background of these I was intentional in the BE-SEE-FLEE-PLEA-BE process, which lasted from three to six months. With each new staff member, it was adjusted and expanded. It was interesting to see the growth in these men as they matured in their faith and their ability.

The first part of the process is observation.

BE:

I wanted these men to be courageous, dedicated teammates but also express their own personalities and passions. During the BE process, each man was given a list of assignments and allowed to work on their own. The first staff member added to UPI was also a part time college student who had a lot on his plate. I observed him working at his own pace, prioritizing work hours and interacting with players. I wanted him to be who he was and develop his own style.

The BE process was followed at different rates with each future staff member. Some were given assignments like writing and creating Bible studies, but they were intentionally not told how to do their job. There were office Bible studies and times of fellowship, but they were given freedom to work in their own style while they were being casually observed.

SEE:

After a few months of the BE process, I began to SEE what really motivated each team member. I was able to observe which projects rose to the top of their lists. I watched to see when their eyes lit up and I observed which tasks they performed with passion. It was exciting to watch them grow into what they were designed to be, and it helped evaluate where they best fit in the ministry. The goal was to empower them to put their personal stamp on their division of the ministry.

Part of the SEE process was allowing for mistakes. I'm not afraid of mistakes, as long as they are not million dollar mistakes! The SEE process allowed me to observe how staff responded to mistakes and learned from them. It also allowed me to observe how each one managed their time. Busyness does not always indicate productivity. It might be masking fear or boredom. *Sometimes activity is just an attempt at artificial significance.*

The SEE process was a time of observing the following:

- How did they handle times of inactivity?
- How did they handle stress?
- How did they respond to adversity?
- How did they manage their time?
- How did they relate to their spouse and/or their children?
- Did they have a need to be in control?
- What was their level of contentment?

- Were they always pushing?
- How did they respond to authority?
- How did they handle their money?
- How did they handle their competitive nature?
- Was integrity one of their core values?
- Were they very opinionated?
- How did they handle opposition?
- How did they handle failure?
- How did they handle success?
- How did they handle their talent?
- Were they arrogant?
- Were they able to work well with others?
- Did they take responsibility for their actions?
- How did they handle discipline?
- What were their spiritual gifts?
- Did they have a servant's heart?
- What was their vision, purpose, and direction?
- What was their personal faith?
- What was their life philosophy?
- Did they have biblical knowledge and maturity?
- Were they a team player or a lone ranger?
- Were they disciplined?
- Were they responsible?
- Did they have a good work ethic?
- What was their temperament?
- What was their communication style?
- What were their spiritual gifts?

FLEE:

After a few months of **BE** and **SEE,** I would intentionally arrange my schedule to be away for a period of time, either at a conference or an international trip. It was time to see what they were made of! Typically, situations would come up while I was away, and the staff member had to make decisions on his own. Often it was a new situation and a decision had to be made with no guidance. Keep in mind, at that time there were no cell phones, laptops or social media apps, and long distance calls were expensive, especially overseas! The individual would need to resolve a situation based on their understanding of Scripture and their understanding of themselves.

PLEA:

This part of the process happened when I returned. We would meet, discuss how things went and what could be learned. It was a time of humbly coming alongside to teach, correct and build up. If there was failure, it was a time to encourage them to get back in the boat. Most importantly, it was a time to discuss why I left and remind them of my desire to have their DNA on everything they did. They needed to see they could run their division on their own.

BE:

At this point, they were free to BE. With a better understanding of who they were and how they best functioned, they were encouraged to be an original; not a copy.

Dr Chris Young, a good friend, offered me some valuable feedback. At the back of my first book, *Released,* I included my BE-SEE-FLEE-PLEA-BE process. He said what he saw was:

- Hands on
- Hands with
- Hands off

Hands ON means training for them to learn about UPI and develop their skills.

HANDS WITH means I'm nearby but not holding their hand.

HANDS OFF means they are free to be who they were designed to be.

You may be wondering if the new member of your flock can seek your advice during this process. Of course! They need to know you are there for them. However, I strongly encourage leaders to expect team members to make an appointment when they want your advice. It demonstrates courtesy and respect for the leader's time. It also causes them to evaluate if it is necessary to seek your advice or if they can handle the situation on their own.

At the completion of the BE-SEE-FLEE-PLEA-BE

process, you will have a better understanding of your sheep and how each one fits into the flock. You will have confidence to challenge them to be who they are and become what they are supposed to be.

This process is not abandonment; it's empowerment. It allows them to grow as people. Some sheep will require more of your time than others but the weaning process has to occur to bring them to true maturity. They need to learn to listen to the voice of the Chief Shepherd.

I'm aware this process may not be practical in every situation, but it worked well for UPI. The men grew strong and became leaders who took ownership in their positions. The risk with this process is developing a *solo mentality*. Working alone can create an attitude of independence rather than team-mindedness. There was risk, but the reward was worth it. They put their fingerprints on the work.

In 2019, after 38 years, I retired from leadership with UPI to follow God's leading in other pursuits. In my years of leadership, there were times of dysfunction between the shepherd and the sheep, but God was developing all of us. I am so grateful for the great team currently leading the organization. The president is demonstrating excellent leadership, and the men and women of UPI are a solid team. I praise God for that!

Mid-Book Jokes

Congratulations! You've made it half way through the book.

EWE NEED A LAUGH.

I thought about writing a book on sheep. But they kept moving so I decided to write it on paper.

People are shocked when they discover I'm a terrible electrician.

I fell off a twenty-foot ladder. Fortunately I was only on the first rung.

I'm into fitness. I'm fittin' this entire cake into my mouth.

I love avocados. But I'd like to ask the manufacturer to put different toys inside. I keep getting wooden balls.

8

WOLVES

KING DAVID WAS A SHEPHERD. He was a shepherd of sheep until God called him to shepherd people. However, even a shepherd king has to watch out for wolves.

Absalom was one of King David's sons. Absalom hated his half-brother Amnon for raping his sister Tamar, and was angry his father did not punish Amnon. Absalom killed Amnon and later led a rebellion against his father, the king, and drove him out of Jerusalem. Here is what scriptures say about him:

> "In all Israel there was not a man so highly praised for his handsome appearance as Absalom. From the top of his head to the sole of his foot there was no blemish in him. Whenever he cut the hair of his head—he used to cut his hair once a year because it became too heavy for him—he would weigh it, and its weight was two hundred shekels by the royal standard." (2 Samuel 14:25-26 NIV)

"In the course of time, Absalom provided himself with a chariot and horses and with fifty men to run ahead of him. He would get up early and stand by the side of the road leading to the city gate. Whenever anyone came with a complaint to be placed before the king for a decision, Absalom would call out to him, 'What town are you from?' He would answer, 'Your servant is from one of the tribes of Israel.' Then Absalom would say to him, 'Look, your claims are valid and proper, but there is no representative of the king to hear you.' And Absalom would add, 'If only I were appointed judge in the land! Then everyone who has a complaint or case could come to me and I would see that they receive justice.'" (2 Samuel 15:1-4 NIV)

In your organization, you may encounter an Absalom or two along the way. They are the wolves who for some reason turn against your leadership. They may even come from within your flock. This is tough. If this happens it is important to understand that Absalom became who he was, in part, because of David. Leaders are not perfect and sometimes their actions or lack of actions will breed an Absalom. Leaders need to accept that truth. If the Holy Spirit reveals where they are responsible, leaders need to adjust their actions accordingly.

Imagine you are King David and your own son attempts to overthrow your leadership. To David's credit, he decided to let God handle the situation. We read in 2 Samuel God used a tree to stop Absalom. God doesn't always intervene in that way. Leaders need to seek direction from Scripture and prayer, remembering God can teach us through these experiences. If you encounter an Absalom, don't become so obsessed you forget about the rest of the flock.

What if the sheep is just a runaway? Shouldn't a shepherd leader go after it to bring it back? Sometimes. Luke 15 records the parable of the shepherd leaving the flock to go after the lost sheep. If someone from your flock is lost or wounded, go after it and work on restoration. But if the sheep bites you, let it go. It will probably infect the whole flock.

> "Everyone is needed, but no one is necessary."
>
> BRUCE COSLET

There is no easy answer when it comes to loyalty. Leadership is sometimes painful and requires painful decisions. Don't allow the terrorist to take all your attention and neglect the loyalist. The flock is the shepherd leader's first responsibility, and neglect makes them vulnerable to wolves. Sometimes the leader needs to let Absolom go. Be ready to be maligned and misunderstood.

In times of distress, remember Jesus is your defense attorney. People may slander you or cause others to question you. You can't control that. I remember going to the trial of a man in trouble with the law who was most likely going to get jail time. As this man entered the courtroom, he acknowledged me and seemed encouraged that I was there. The trial began and the prosecutor stated his case to the judge. Meanwhile, the man I had come to see was continually whispering into the ear of his attorney. Suddenly, his attorney loudly told him to stop talking and let him do his job! I got his point. I have been guilty of trying to defend myself. I believe Jesus would prefer I would be quiet and let him do his job.

Shepherd leader, let Jesus defend you against rumors and false information that you cannot control. I once saw this written on a white board:

> "When a toxic person can no longer control you, they will try to control how others see you. The misinformation will feel unfair, but stay above it, trusting that other people will eventually see the truth, just like you did."

Even better, here is what the Chief Shepherd says:

> "Do not take revenge, my dear friends, but leave room for God's wrath, for it is written: 'It is mine to avenge; I will repay,' says the Lord." (Romans 12:19 NIV)

9

EDUCATION

"Save Your people and bless Your inheritance; be their shepherd also and carry them forever." (Psalm 28:9 ESV)

SHEPHERD LEADERS NEVER STOP LEARNING

ANY DISCUSSION about leadership needs to include the importance of continuing education. Society is always changing. Traditions and technology continue to evolve. Shepherd leaders need to keep up so they don't have to catch up. The current generation is the first to grow up with social media, and parents are scrambling to navigate this uncharted territory. Change is relentless.

"Leaders need to stay ready so they don't have to get ready!"

Late in my career with UPI, I was privileged to study under professional counselor and author, Jerry Price. We studied several hours a day, four days a week for eight weeks. He would instruct, evaluate, correct, and encourage me. What I learned was life-changing. During this time together we developed a deep relationship and eventually authored four books together. Cancer claimed Jerry on December 7, 2018, but his legacy lives on through me and many others he taught.

His book *Transforming Twisted Thinking* was our textbook for the eight weeks. The premise is that we are all twisted in our thinking. So much of counseling focuses on behavior modification, but Jerry maintains if our thinking doesn't change, we will eventually revert to unhealthy behavior. The time studying with Jerry helped me understand why I acted like I did, and it also gave me leadership tools for shepherding my flock as a father, a coach and a leader of a ministry.

T.E.A. Thinking determines Emotion, Emotion determines Action

The following are the ten thinking errors that Jerry identifies in his book which will provide a basic understanding for future leaders. For more detailed information, *Transforming Twisted Thinking* by Jerry Price is available on Amazon.com.

TEN THINKING ERRORS *from Transforming Twisted Thinking by Jerry Price:*

1. CLOSED THINKING:

"Closed Thinking is a choice to be non-receptive to others where there's an unwillingness to hear, listen, or consider people while maintaining personal agendas that promote a Big E (Excitement of the forbidden)."

- A. I Am Not Receptive (tunnel vision-the only way is how I see things)
- B. I Am Not Self Critical (Emotionally vacant—I don't care how I hurt others)
- C. I Am Not Disclosing Information (Deliberately vague, no details)
- D. I Am Good At Pointing Out and Talking About Other's Faults
- E. I Lie by Omission

2. MARTYRED THINKING:

- A. I view myself as a victim when held accountable
- B. I blame social conditions, my family, the past and others for what I do

3. INFLATED THINKING:

- A. I view myself only as a good person to avoid responsibility for offenses
- B. I fail to acknowledge my own destructive behavior
- C. I build myself up at the expense of others

4. STUBBORN THINKING:

- A. I won't give any effort to do things I find boring or disagreeable
- B. When I say "I can't" I am really saying "I won't"

5. RECKLESS THINKING:

- A. I think living in a responsible way is unexciting and unsatisfying
- B. I have no sense of obligation, but I will get you to obligate yourself to me
- C. I am not interested in being responsible unless I get an immediate payoff

6. IMPATIENT THINKING:

- A. I do not use the past as a learning tool when it gets in the way of my plans

- B. I expect others to act immediately when I demand it of them
- C. I make decisions based on assumptions and not the facts

7. ZERO THINKING:

- A. I have irrational fears but refuse to admit them
- B. I have a fundamental fear of injury or death when I am not in control
- C. I have a profound fear of being put down
- D. When I am held accountable, I feel lousy and experience a *zero* state

8. MANIPULATIVE THINKING:

- A. I have a compelling need to be in control of others and situations
- B. I use manipulation and deceit to be in and take control of situations
- C. I refuse to be a dependent person, unless I can take advantage of it

9. ARROGANT THINKING:

- A. I think I am better and different than others

- B. I expect out of others what I fail to meet
- C. I am super optimistic because it cuts my fear of failure
- D. I will quit at the first sign of failure

10. POSSESSIVE THINKING:

"An Ownership Attitude." This is an attitude "of looking at all things and people as objects to possess."

- A. I perceive all things and people as objects that belong to me
- B. I have no concept of the "ownership rights" of others
- C. I will use "sex" for power and control and not intimacy

Jerry had a huge impact on my leadership style and thinking.

S.T.A.R. Straight Thinkers Accept Responsibility

Another book on leadership that I highly recommend is *Tale of Three Kings* by Gene Edwards. The entire UPI staff read it. The book is short but has some great insights into leadership styles.

I believe Shepherd Leaders need a keen understanding of how to think and process life. We need to be healthy and strong in truth and use that stability to care for our flock and understand how they think as well. When we are mature and healthy as leaders we can reach more deeply into the thinking of individuals in our sphere of influence.

It takes time to know ourselves and our flock, and sometimes it is painful. The way we approach the subject of thinking patterns is important. An illustration I like comes from the world of golf. The golfer does not hit the ball before he sees where it lies. The location determines which club to choose.

I have sometimes been guilty of impatience and used a driver when a putter was sufficient. Not all situations require the same tools. Understand how people think, where they lie and how they respond before you decide how to approach them.

SPIRITUAL GIFTS

Shepherd leaders need to help their flock discover their spiritual gifts. These are not the same as talents. Gifts are given for the purpose of building up the flock and advancing the kingdom of God. Many people are unaware of their spiritual gifts but according to Scripture, the Holy Spirit has gifted every believer. Guiding your flock into working in their area of giftedness will empower them and benefit your organization.

To assist in determining spiritual gifts, there are free tests available on the internet. A great group exercise is to ask the members of your flock to identify which gifts they see in each other.

DELEGATION

Delegating is an important and ongoing process. Leaders often find themselves trying to do everything. Sometimes it seems much easier to do it yourself than take the time to train others. Leaders know how to do it and they know how they want it done. It isn't easy to delegate and allow others to do things their own way, but it's necessary. If not, the leader will burn out and the flock will feel unnecessary. Delegation also builds trust. If your flock feels you don't trust them, you will stunt their growth. And if you don't show you trust them, they will have a hard time trusting your leadership.

- Clarify what matters to you
- Stop doing things that matter less and focus on things in your area of giftedness
- Allow others to do what they enjoy to free you up to lead and help them grow.

"Teach me your way, O Lord, that I may walk in your truth; unite my heart to fear your name. I give thanks to you, O Lord my God, with my whole heart, and I will glorify your name forever. For great is your steadfast love toward me; you have delivered my soul from the depths of Sheol." (Psalms 86:11-13 ESV)

"Success is not always what you have achieved but what you become."

10

R.E.A.L.

"Be shepherds of God's flock that is under your care, watching over them—not because you must, but because you are willing, as God wants you to be; not pursuing dishonest gain, but eager to serve; not lording it over those entrusted to you, but being examples to the flock. And when the Chief Shepherd appears, you will receive the crown of glory that will never fade away." (1 Peter 5:2-4 NIV)

THE R.E.A.L ACROSTIC: RESPONSIVE. ENGAGED. AUTHENTIC. LOYAL.

THE NEXT FOUR chapters will focus on the R.E.A.L. acrostic. But first, I'd like to talk briefly about the word *remain*. Leadership is an honor, but it is also a huge responsibility. I know it's often too much for me and I'm pretty sure you feel the same. The good news is that we don't have to shoulder the load alone. We are invited into partnership.

> *"Shepherd leadership requires staying connected to the Chief Shepherd."*

"I am the vine; you are the branches. If you remain in me and I in you, you will bear much fruit; apart from me you can do nothing." (John 15:5 NIV)

Jesus calls himself the vine, and he makes it pretty clear how important it is to stay connected. Basically, if we want to be productive, we have to stay connected. If we disconnect we will accomplish nothing.

How do we stay connected? We *remain*. What I see in John 15 is shepherd leaders need to:

GAZE, GRAZE and PRAISE.

Gaze: Meditate on all the Lord has done for you. He prepared you and placed you and provided for you. See his hand in each step. Think about all he has taught you. Remember all the ways he has blessed you. Remind yourself he has a plan for your life. Gaze at his goodness.

Graze: Feed your soul from God's Word. Information is coming at you from all directions. Make sure it lines up with his perspective. Nourish your heart and mind. There is something cleansing and refreshing about Scripture. It's like taking a daily brain bath. Keep in mind God has promised his Word will always accomplish its intended purpose.

Praise: Worship looks different for each of us. Whatever it takes for you—gratitude, prayer, music, a walk in the woods—turn your focus to God's greatness.

Leaders do not have to become shepherd leaders alone. If God has called you to be a leader and you desire to lead like the Chief Shepherd, stay connected. He will form shepherd leadership in you.

Hang on tight and let's take a look at R.E.A.L. leadership. Responsive, engaged, authentic and loyal.

11

RESPONSIVE

"Let your speech always be with grace, as though seasoned with salt, so that you will know how you should respond to each person." (Colossians 4:6 NASB)

A SHEPHERD LEADER has to be looking and listening to be able to respond. It takes time to read the temperature of a flock. Watch the body language. Watch how they interact with each other. Ask questions. Listen to what they are saying. Be available.

Being responsive is more than telling others what to do. It's about being perceptive to needs and responding to them. It's about discerning the talents and abilities within your flock. It's about paying attention to the emotional health of the flock.

Responsive shepherd leaders do more listening than talking. They encourage their flock to share their thoughts and they listen carefully. When people are treated with respect and believe they matter to the organization, it's amazing how this energizes them to work well together toward a common goal.

When problems surface, and they will, the shepherd leader addresses them by creating a culture where it is safe to air grievances and work to resolve them. Ignoring problems will not make them go away. The result of dealing with problems as they come up will be a team that functions well together.

Something that has been helpful to me when dealing with others to resolve conflict is to ask myself how I would treat this person if they were one of my parents. I know I would use a respectful tone.

Keep in mind it is not always the role of the shepherd leader to resolve issues within the flock. Sometimes the leader needs to allow the flock to resolve their problems themselves. It is one of the most important ways for them to grow as a team. However, a good shepherd leader is available and responsive when needed.

Responsive shepherd leaders know that timing is very important. Sometimes it is wise to wait before responding. It may be wise to allow emotions to cool down. Responding out of emotion is usually not productive. I have tried to develop the habit of writing down my response and setting it aside. After taking time to think and pray is always a better time to revisit, revise and respond.

Sometimes the issues are not the real issues. Your flock may be dealing with situations you are not aware of, which may come to the surface if you are patient. Be intentional but aware of the right timing.

"Step back before you come back so you don't cause a setback!"

I'll never forget a comment I heard years ago while coaching at a small college. We were playing a Division One team on their field. Their coach and I met at home plate to exchange lineup cards for the game. As we waited for the umpires, he brought up another coach we both knew and he said, "He's only about the X's and O's. I thought about that comment on the way back to the dugout and I've thought about it many times since. The X's and O's are important. They represent the day to day responsibilities of coaching or leading a flock. But leading is about much more than the daily X's and O's. Shepherd leadership is about listening, hearing and responding in the context of a caring relationship. It's about the flock.

WHAT WAS MOST IMPORTANT TO ME AS I ATTEMPTED TO BE RESPONSIVE?

As I've taught on being a responsive shepherd leader, I've narrowed down a list of what I consider important:

1. A shepherd leader needs to understand the *power of the positive*. We need to be realistic; not everything is positive. But we can always find

something positive in an individual or a situation if we look for it.
2. *To compare is an error.* Comparing ourselves with others can lead to unhealthy attitudes or unhealthy competition. We should strive for personal best.
3. *Be on time.* Being late steals time from others. It is a form of selfishness which says my time is more important than yours. Philippians chapter 2 encourages us to value others above ourselves.
4. *Develop a critical eye.* A critical eye is not the same as a critical spirit. A critical eye can spot a problem and will take the initiative to deal with it. A critical eye can see the potential in people. A critical spirit *blames, defames* and *shames*.
5. *Build trust.* Trust takes a long time to build and it can be destroyed quickly. Shepherd leaders seek to build trust within the flock, and they start by setting the example. It saddens me to realize I have probably broken trust at times by responding too quickly and not taking time to analyze the situation. Your flock will not follow you if they don't believe they can trust you.
6. *Lead with courage.* A shepherd leader must be willing to step into the unknown. Part of leading is taking a risk and being willing to own the consequences.
7. *Be humble.* Shepherd leaders must be humble enough to realize they don't have all the answers

and they won't always respond well. Taking responsibility for wrong responses is part of leadership. There is power in an apology.

Allow me to relate a story that illustrates this.

When I was a young college coach I took my team on a spring trip to Hawaii. During a game with the University of Hilo, I became irate at the umpire and did not respond well. I did not feel he was calling a fair game and I let him know it. I ran onto the field, yelled in his face, and knocked him over!

After the game, when I had cooled down, I knew what I had to do. I had blown it in front of my team, the opposing team and all the fans. I went to the home team locker room and asked the coach if I could speak to his team. He looked at me suspiciously but agreed. I asked the coach, the team, and the umpires to forgive me for the way I had acted. Then I asked my team for forgiveness as well.

Later, their third baseman came up to me and hugged me, saying he had never seen anything like that. Before the next game, the head coach said to me, "I don't know what religion you are, but I want to know more." There is power in an apology.

Build a responsive team.

Responsive shepherd leaders look for responsive team members. They look for men and women of integrity, courage, humility and character as well as proficiency in their job. They reinforce the qualities of responsive leadership in their flock. It is better if the sheep don't always agree with the leader. One of my weaknesses is I like to be liked. That can lead to making decisions that are popular with the flock but may not be the best long term decision for the organization. It is healthy to have team members who are willing to respectfully disagree.

Shepherd leaders need to model healthy responses, nurture and expect the same in their flock.

12

ENGAGED

"Then Jesus told them this parable: 'Suppose one of you has a hundred sheep and loses one of them. Doesn't he leave the ninety-nine in the open country and go after the lost sheep until he finds it? And when he finds it, he joyfully puts it on his shoulders and goes home. Then he calls his friends and neighbors together and says, 'Rejoice with me; I have found my lost sheep.'" (Luke 15:3-6 NIV)

HOW DOES a shepherd leader engage on a daily basis? By being intentional about the needs of each member of the flock. Below are several practical ways to flesh this out.

ASK QUESTIONS

It's amazing what you can learn by asking a simple question. The next time you meet with someone in your flock, try a question like this: "What can I do to make you more successful?"

We've already discussed the importance of your flock's fingerprints on everything they do, but that doesn't mean you aren't available to help. Asking good questions is one way a shepherd leader can be proactive about engaging with the flock.

LISTEN

Another way to engage is to schedule meetings with your flock solely for the purpose of listening. It may take time to build trust before individuals are comfortable opening up with you or with each other. But once they see you care and that you are truly *listening*, they will feel safe to speak up about their ideas, problems and needs. Creating a climate of trust takes time and effort, but once it happens, it will be much easier to keep a finger on the pulse of your flock and stay engaged.

FACE TIME

There were many years I traveled extensively with UPI. The technology we have today was not available, and communication with the staff was almost impossible. Because of that, we developed a routine of staff meetings when I got back to the office. There is nothing like a face to face meeting, not just for information but for relationships. I had missed them and wanted to get together. While we updated each other, relationships grew deeper.

There are only so many hours in a day and you have work that has to get done. I understand. Work would pile up whenever I was away, which was often. You may feel you can't afford to take the time for meetings like this. I want to tell you, you can't afford *not* to take the time. For me, it meant some of my work had to be done during flights or at home. Dedicate time to engage with your flock, so they know they matter to you. The payoff is huge.

When people know they are valued there is harmony in the flock and work is more pleasant. Most of the time, meeting with my staff was enjoyable. These were great times discussing our mission, setting goals, sharing stories and catching up. Naturally, issues occasionally came up which had to be discussed and resolved. Evaluations can cause tension. That's normal, but those uncomfortable conversations are received much better when the relationships are strong. There is less uncertainty, insecurity, and unhealthy competition. A cohesive flock can work through tough topics and come out stronger.

As the ministry of UPI grew, it became obvious it was time to branch out from the midwest office and establish satellite offices in areas that were baseball hubs, beginning with the South and the Southwest. It was the right thing to do, but it exposed the holes in my leadership.

I had a lot to learn about communication when face to face meetings were not possible. Part of my continuing education as a leader was discovering that communication by phone and email was not enough. I needed to be physically present with each one at least twice a year to stay engaged.

EXTENDED FAMILY

Shepherd leaders have a heart for their flock that extends beyond the workplace. They care about the personal lives and the families of those under their care. They celebrate life's milestones like birthdays, anniversaries, and graduations, and they are involved during the tough times, such as the loss of a loved one. In other words, your flock is extended family and part of shepherd leadership is engaging with your flock outside of work.

LONG MATH

Sometimes being engaged means exposing pain in your flock, but engaging means more than simply exposing pain. None of us gets to glide through life without being wounded somehow. Shepherd leaders need to be willing to do the "long math." What do I mean by that? When I was learning math in grade school, some problems were easier than others and I knew the correct answer right away.

But the teacher required us to do the long math. That used to upset me. If I had the right answer, what difference did it make? The teacher wanted to see the process to see *how I got there.* The Shepherd Leader may need to engage in the process of understanding the source of the pain and walking together toward restoration.

PRAYER

Have you ever told someone you would pray for them and promptly forgot? Me too. That's why I recommend asking if they mind if you pray right then and there. I can't think of a better way to stay engaged with your flock than to ask them, "How can I pray for you?" There is something about praying together that softens and calms anxious sheep.

INTENT vs. IMPACT

There is a difference between intent and impact. You may have the right intentions about being more engaged, but what you are doing, or not doing, is not having the impact you intended. Being engaged may take a bit of trial and error. Or it may simply take time. Be intentional about engaging and don't give up. Your flock is worth it.

> *"Efficiency is getting things done right. Effectiveness is getting the right things done."*

Shepherd leadership is messy, and being an engaged shepherd leader is even messier. It's not easy and it requires you to be all in. But that is how Jesus calls us to lead. He entered into the mess of our lives and he is engaged with us. As much as you are able, and as much as you are allowed, engage with your flock.

13

AUTHENTIC

"Do not be afraid, little flock, for your Father has chosen gladly to give you the kingdom. (Luke 12:32)

WHAT IS AUTHENTIC LEADERSHIP? And how does a leader go about being authentic? Two simple words: *be you.*

That's what authentic means. It means people get the genuine you, blemishes and all. You are an open book with no hidden agenda. You are not afraid people will see your flaws because you don't try to hide them. You are growing as a leader and that means you are not perfect and you will never be perfect. That's humbling but it's good. There is something incredibly freeing about living and leading this way. It gives other people permission to be authentic as well. God has trusted you, an imperfect shepherd, to be perfectly authentic.

Norm Wilhelmi, one of my spiritual mentors, taught me it was ok to be myself. He took me on a journey out of religiosity and into authenticity. He taught me not to hide my personality and my sense of humor. He was a model of authenticity and I will always be grateful for his example. Where did we get the idea we have to be perfect, anyway? God does not expect you to fit into anyone else's mold. He designed you to be unique, so don't be afraid to be the leader you were created to be. No one else has your exact set of interests and abilities, so don't hide them. Accepting your position of leadership, openly admitting your shortcomings, is authenticity at its finest. The Chief Shepherd will not stop working on you, chiseling away at your imperfections and sculpting you into the shepherd leader he designed you to be.

Be you.

There's really no point trying to hide your imperfections anyway. Your flock already knows and they will appreciate your authenticity. As the leader, you set the tone by being real, admitting when you are wrong, and taking the initiative to change. Authentic humility is refreshing and there is a pretty good chance your flock will follow your example.

AUTHENTIC GOAL SETTING

Part of authenticity is transparency. Be clear about your goals and your expectations so your flock knows which flags to salute. Define what success looks like. If your flock does not know what a win looks like, they will have to figure it out on their own, and they may end up headed in a different direction than you intended. Don't be vague or ambiguous. Set measurable standards and deadlines.

One of my earliest coaching jobs was junior varsity basketball coach at a small, rural school. There were a couple of young men on my team with athletic talent, but most of the kids were farm kids with exceptional work ethic. Part way into the season, the varsity coach tagged the most talented kids for his team and things did not look good for the rest of the JV team's season. Second string players were now starters. In an attempt to motivate them, I told my team if they won thirteen games, I would buy them all a steak dinner. Guess what? They won thirteen games and no more! Set your goals, make them clear, and watch your team succeed.

Shepherd leaders need to know what they believe and authentically live their beliefs. Hopefully you have a mission statement for your organization. Do you have a personal mission statement yet? If not, I recommend thinking it through and writing it down now, because it will help you live consistently and authentically. Your flock deserves a leader who lives what he or she believes, and they will find it easy to follow someone who knows their mission.

AUTHENTIC VALUES

A shepherd leader values more than recognition or financial success. These things are not wrong, but they are temporary. Shepherd leaders keep their eyes on the eternal. Shepherd leadership is about following the Chief Shepherd in what he has called us to do. That is our purpose; our core value. That determines how we do what we do. Authentic shepherd leadership means not allowing the opinions of others to determine our direction. We listen to others, but ultimately, we work for an audience of One.

> *"We work for an audience of One."*

Once the flock understands the values of the organization, they will add value. Remember, you saw something in them when you hired them, and you have the honor of cultivating what you saw in them. Let them know you value them. Don't assume they already know. Give them the freedom to be themselves, and don't expect them to do things exactly like you. Don't be surprised if they find better ways to get things done. Articulate your values, nurture your flock, encourage their individuality.

AUTHENTIC OPENNESS

There is a difference between *honesty* and *openness*. Being honest means I'm telling you the truth. Being open means telling you the whole truth; the full story. For example, I can be truthful and tell you I was working, but fail to be open about my attitude toward my work. Authenticity is both honest and open. Openness requires being vulnerable and it will take time before your flock is willing to take a risk on being open. Creating a climate of openness will require receptiveness and respect. The shepherd leader must understand the responsibility involved.

AUTHENTICITY WITH INTENT AND IMPACT

As we have already discussed, there is a difference between *intent* and *impact*. We may not *intend* to hurt someone but the *impact* of our words or actions have the potential to offend. For example, maybe you spoke harshly to someone. Maybe you were in a hurry and did not intend to offend, but you came across as angry. Authenticity means shepherd leaders need to be alert to unintentional offenses. Addressing them openly and apologizing if you caused the offense creates an opportunity to clear the air and speak life into your flock.

AUTHENTICITY IN PAIN

Sometimes the shepherd leader will get hurt. People say hurtful things. Projects fail. A friend betrays you. Sometimes the pain is deep but pain is a great teacher. I don't believe it is helpful to ignore the pain or act like it doesn't hurt. Authenticity means being vulnerable with your flock and allowing them to see your pain. You may wrestle with the reasons that have caused your pain, and you may have a sleepless night or two. That's ok, but be careful not to react out of the pain because your flock is watching you and will learn from the way you respond. Take time to pray and allow the Chief Shepherd to align your attitude with His before responding. That is part of leadership.

The gift of pain is that God brings good from it. Pain is a great teacher. God uses pain to shape us into better leaders. We become more compassionate and we learn how to walk with others through their pain.

> "And we know that all that happens to us is working for our good if we love God and are fitting into his plans." (Romans 8:28, TLB)

14

LOYALTY

> "He makes me lie down in green pastures; He leads me beside quiet waters. He restores my soul; He guides me in the paths of righteousness For His name's sake." (Psalm 23:2-3)

GOD IS LOYAL. He takes incredibly good care of us and provides what we need. How can shepherd leaders integrate loyalty into their flock? By faithfully representing the heart of God. Loyalty to the flock means providing the training, the support, and the leadership needed. One of the best ways to represent the heart of God is to speak what is good and helpful.

Shepherd leaders have the opportunity to use words for positive influence. There is enough negative talk around us and your flock doesn't need negativity from you. Even when confronting problems, the loyal leader is thinking of how his words will benefit the flock.

"Do not let any unwholesome talk come out of your mouths, but **only what is helpful for building others up according to their needs,** that it may benefit those who listen." (Ephesians 4:29 NIV)

"Therefore **encourage one another** and **build each other up** as you are already doing…" (Philippians 2:4)

LOYALTY IN CONFIDENCES

Loyal shepherd leaders know how to keep a confidence and they need to let their flock know they expect the same from them. I can't stress this point enough. Protecting information shared in confidence is a high priority. Unfortunately, many leaders do not take this seriously and the relational damage is difficult to overcome. Loyalty means it is essential not to break a trust. If you want your flock to trust you, you need to be known as someone who knows how to keep a confidence.

This does not cancel the importance of openness and vulnerability. The difference is shepherd leaders are personally open and vulnerable, but they must protect information others have shared with them in confidence. Leaders who encourage openness and vulnerability in their flock do not have the right to share what they have heard with anyone else. Mature leaders know that things shared in confidence should never be used to advance their own agenda. Confidences must be protected.

LOYALTY IN RELATIONSHIPS

Loyalty in relationships goes beyond family and close friends. Loyalty means if I have a problem with someone, I go directly to that person to deal with the issue. Unfortunately, most of us tend to talk about the issue with other people, creating something called triangulation. We have brought another person into the relationship and complicated the problem. This is disloyal and can easily become slander, damaging a person's reputation. A shepherd leader has the courage to go directly to the individual without involving others.

> "Brothers and sisters do not slander one another." (James 4:11 NIV)

LOYALTY IN CONFLICT

> "Life with God is not immunity from difficulties, but peace in difficulties."
>
> C. S. LEWIS

Shepherd leaders are problem solvers. Conflicts will come. Ideally, a healthy flock has learned how to handle conflict on their own. When that is not possible, hopefully your flock will feel safe bringing it to you. Stay positive, calm, and level headed. Ask questions and listen carefully to each side. Pray for wisdom and avoid making decisions until you have all the facts. God is pleased when we ask for his wisdom.

> "If any of you lacks wisdom, you should ask God, who gives generously to all without finding fault, and it will be given to you." (James 1:5)

Resolving conflict is an important part of leadership. Healthy conflict resolution can set a positive tone and create unity in the flock. The shepherd leader fosters loyalty within the flock by refusing to allow conflict to divide but using it as an opportunity to reinforce relationships.

Maybe the conflict is between you and one of your flock. Timing is important. I suggest asking the individual if it is a good time to discuss the issue. Asking permission gives some power back to the individual and shows you value them and their time.

Don't allow the discussion to get personal; keep it about the conflict. Don't allow emotion to take over. Keep an open mind; you might learn something valuable. If you are responsible for even part of the conflict, be the first to ask for forgiveness. Even if you handle everything well, there is no guarantee how the other person will respond. You may not reach a resolution, but you can be respectful. You can have peace knowing you did everything in your power to resolve the conflict.

LOYALTY IN FAILURE

Failure is a great classroom. You win some and you learn some. Shepherd leaders remain loyal through failure and press through.

In American football, when a defensive lineman is blocked he knows to fight against the pressure because that is the exact place the ball is going to go. Leaders need to fight against pressure and not give up. Pressure may come from people or processes. It may come from circumstances you can't control. Have the courage to fight against the pressure even when it's painful.

This book is being written during a global pandemic without equal in our lifetime. Leaders all around the world are facing unfathomable pressure. Some will rise to the occasion; some will not. Stay loyal and stay in the fight.

LOYALTY IN CHARACTER

Character is who you are when no one is looking. Character sets the standard high and is loyal to the standard. Loyalty understands character is more important than reputation. You can't control others who try to destroy your reputation, but you can control if it is true or not. Take the high road and eventually the truth will come out. Remember, God is your defender.

Loyalty trusts in the character of others, giving them the benefit of the doubt. Take every opportunity to encourage character in others.

LOYALTY IN SOLITUDE

Shepherd leaders are called to a higher standard, and none of us can live up to this standard by ourselves. If the Chief Shepherd required times of solitude, so do shepherd leaders. We need to be intentional about time for reading, listening, reflection and prayer. We need to seek God's wisdom and counsel, strength and perspective.

Some of my best times of solitude were on long flights like Asia, Africa or Australia. Other times were in lonely hotel rooms far from home. By far the best time is daily time in God's Word, allowing it to soak in, reflecting on it and listening for the Holy Spirit. Quiet times with Jesus are always a good investment!

You can spend your life anywhere, but where will you invest it?

Loyalty is an investment in people. Leaders who don't invest in their staff betray them and risk losing good people. Their staff will lose trust, hope, and motivation. They will lose their passion for the vision of the organization. They will lose unity and productivity. The opportunity to develop them into leaders will be lost.

The greatest risk for disloyal leaders may be to themselves. They have not been loyal to their calling and they have missed the opportunity to walk the people of their flock into their divine destiny.

Shepherd leadership isn't easy but the returns are huge.

People are hungry for genuine relationships. They need to know they have value beyond fulfilling assignments. Most of us have multiple virtual 'friends' and few genuine relationships. Your flock needs responsive, engaging, authentic, loyal leadership.

15

CHALLENGE

SHEPHERD LEADERS UNDERSTAND it is essential to be constantly learning. Books, conferences, classes and podcasts are a few ways to continue educating yourself. If you have one or two useful takeaways from each session it is time well spent. I hope you have gained something useful from this book. The thoughts I've shared have come from a lifetime of learning how to lead. You won't be able to implement everything at once, but it is my hope you have found something of value.

Here are a few final challenges:

- Be authentic
- Keep learning
- Keep growing
- Be a servant
- Love your flock
- Follow the Shepherd

- Stay connected
- Don't be ashamed of your faith

Time is a finite resource. Make today the day you decide to lead like a shepherd.

It's great to be alive, because God is in control!

ABOUT THE AUTHOR

TOM ROY was the founder and president of Unlimited Potential, Inc., a ministry with professional baseball players. He has been a voice in major league baseball for almost four decades. Tom also coached baseball at the high school and college level for eighteen years, and is currently leading *Shepherd Coach Network* (link below). Tom and his wife, Carin, live in Winona Lake, Indiana, and they are the parents of two adult daughters and six grandchildren.

TO CONNECT WITH TOM, VISIT ONLINE OR WRITE TO:

1247 FREEDOM PARKWAY
WINONA LAKE, INDIANA 46590

WWW.**SHEPHERDCOACHNETWORK**.COM

ALSO BY TOM ROY

SHEPHERD COACH

The first installment of the Shepherd Series, a practical workbook for anyone in a position of leadership.

RELEASED

A story of God's Power Released in Pro Baseball

BEYOND BETRAYAL

(co-authored with Jerry Price)

SANDUSKY BAY

(co-authored with Jerry Price)

ELLISON BAY

(co-authored with Jerry Price)

LAKE OF BAYS

(co-authored with Jerry Price)

END NOTES

2. Style

1. https://wisetoast.com/types-of-leadership-styles/
2. Will Kenton

4. Heart

1. The Seasons of the Shepherd

www.ingramcontent.com/pod-product-compliance
Lightning Source LLC
Chambersburg PA
CBHW071418210526
45465CB00001B/446